I love Ecuador & Galapagos Islands
travel guide

By S. L. Giger as *SwissMiss on Tour*

"Don't listen to what they say, go see."
- Chinese Proverb

Receive a free packing list

Never forget anything important ever again and don't waste unnecessary time with packing. Scan the QR code and receive a free packing list along with a sample of my Thailand travel guide.

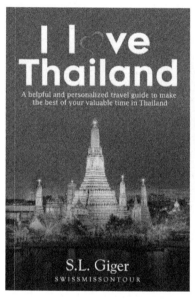

Content

Why should I choose this guidebook instead of any other?

Do you only have a limited amount of time (like two or three weeks) and aren't quite sure which places of Ecuador to fit into your schedule? Do you have doubts about whether you can afford a trip to the Galapagos Islands or how to organize it best? This guidebook will help you to plan your trip and to really focus on the must-sees of Ecuador. Prepare yourself for colorful rain forests with abundant wildlife, thunderous waterfalls, and incredible views from volcanos.

Probably, the usual guidebook which talks about every small city will burst your timeframe. Therefore, you only find the best of the best in *I love Ecuador*, which still could easily fill three weeks to a month, but you can also visit this country in less time.

Do you want to plan your own, smooth journey in Ecuador? This guidebook will make this an easy task.

Before my first trip to Ecuador, I worried about the people not speaking English and about safety in general. I thought I would get robbed, held at gunpoint, and surely be an easy target as a solo female traveler. So, I prepared myself with safety advice (which I also included in this book). My first trip was such a positive experience, that I returned twice to be able to spend more time in this diverse country.

If you read this guidebook, you will get to experience the best of Ecuador without having to do any further research. You find a two-week travel itinerary with detailed "how-to"-guidelines and further ideas and descriptions.

In case you are worried about the Spanish language, there is a small language guide with helpful words at the end of this book. Otherwise, you should be fine with hands, feet, and in seldom cases, Google translate.

Now, it's your turn to go exploring. Vamos!

Reasons to look forward to your journey in Ecuador in case you are not entirely convinced yet

Congratulations! Since you are holding this book in your hands you are probably at least contemplating going to Ecuador. Somehow, it often is an overlooked country when people only have a limited time for a holiday and are choosing between Colombia, Peru, Brazil, or Argentina. However, for the small size of Ecuador in comparison to its neighboring countries, it probably has more highlights on display than the other countries! I hope, that with this travel guide, I can make you feel my love for Ecuador. My enthusiasm for the Salsa music which you hear everywhere, the local chocolate, the rich biodiversity, the helpful people, and the indigenous culture traits that can still be observed today.

In Ecuador, it's possible to watch whales while surfing, hike snow-covered volcanos (also one of the highest active volcanos in South America), spot colorful and exotic birds with your own eyes, ride bicycles to waterfalls, or get pampered in spas or on luxurious cruise ships. Since mainland Ecuador isn't yet as well-known as some of the neighboring countries it isn't yet as overrun, and it would be a good time to visit (in case they aren't protesting at the moment*).

I only spoke a tourist amount of Spanish when I went to Ecuador the first time. Some people speak English, but you will get a much better connection to the locals if you learn the few words in Spanish that I attached at the end of this book. It was always easy to find the information I needed as the people are friendly.

*About the protests: During all the time I spent in Ecuador, I didn't feel anything from the political tensions. Everyone was nice and helpful. Then, the day after I left the country (lucky me) roads were blocked, buildings were lit on fire, and tourists were stuck. So, this quick development came as quite a shock to me. However, since the violence wasn't directed against the tourists, they weren't in danger. It was just annoying for the tourists because they couldn't have their trip as planned and sad for Ecuador that there was no better way to fight against the troubles. The worst time lasted about 11 days and after that it was okay to travel again. So, don't let yourself being stopped because you read something bad on the news about Ecuador. Yes, inform yourself on the government or travel advice page of your country about the current situation of Ecuador. This is important for any country you travel to in South America because situations can change from one day to the other and this guidebook can never be up to date enough. However, even if there are some words of warning online, I can now say out of my own experience, that the troubles (except during those 11 days after the first big eruption in 2019) are usually concentrated to one square in one city and tourists can avoid the protest completely. For example, people were being tear-gassed in Santiago and Valparaiso in Chile, and people protest in Buenos Aires every day and the TV made it look as if the whole country was a war zone. However, my travel route led through those countries during that time. Since I met many other travelers who just came from those places and assured me that it was fine to be there as a tourist, I luckily still went there and had an enjoyable time. Tourists are an important source of income for those countries after all.

Apart from possible political tensions, we now also have to check the current covid regulations. Therefore, there is a special chapter about covid travel advice in this book.

In conclusion, inform yourself about the current travel situation of a country you want to visit (perhaps by contacting a hostel) and stay safe with the safety advice which I included in this travel guide. I'm sure you will have such a great time in Ecuador as I did.

About the author of this guidebook

Seraina loves to travel since she can remember. It started with beach vacations with her family when she was a child but soon, she sought her own routes. She was lucky to be able to spend an amazing High School year in New York when she was 15 years old. Then she started to write her first travel blog which evolved into **SwissMissOnTour** (www.swissmissontour.com). Later, she explored Europe with Interrail but was also attracted by the exotic countries further away. Countless trips to Southeast Asia made her fall in love with the delicious Asian flavors, beautiful temples, and natural highlights. South America was always at the back of her mind but for that, she wanted to have more time in order not to have to fly back and forth to Switzerland in every vacation. So, when the timing was right, she quit her job and since then is fully enjoying the countries of South America. As she was writing this, she was sitting in a café in Buenos Aires, still enjoying every minute of this great journey.

Ecuador Highlights

I am surprised at how many people skip Ecuador on their South America trip as there is such a high concentration of highlights in this comparatively small country. Here are my three favorites from the mainland. The Galapagos Islands are added as a bonus at the end of the book and the whole trip there was a highlight as it's incredible how many different wild animals you get to see and how they aren't bothered about humans getting close to them.

1 Cotopaxi Volcano

Be impressed by the red-brown volcano with the snow tip. Whether you attempt this high altitude climb or observe it from afar, it looks stunning against the blue sky.

2 Whale Watching in Puerto Lopez

Usually, whale watching involves a long journey and a whole day on the boat to perhaps see a fin of a whale. However, if you are in Ecuador between June and  September you can hop on a small boat at the port of Puerto Lopez and within twenty minutes you will be surrounded by at least two whales. On many days, you can see whales from any beach along the coast, but the boat helps you to see every detail of this magnificent animal.

3 Pailón del Diablo, Baños

 I also really loved watching hummingbirds in the tranquil forest of Mindo but as a true waterfall lover, I have to add this amazing waterfall onto the highlights list. It's very touristy but also an adventurous attraction.

Things to consider before you visit Ecuador to have the best possible trip

In this chapter, you find all the information you need to know for a smooth journey in Ecuador.

Currency

Ecuador uses the US-Dollar. The short form is USD. In case your country doesn't use the USD, you can find out the current conversion rate by, for example, typing AUD to USD into the Google search bar.

It's not common to pay with a credit card. Therefore, bring small bills of $5, $10, and $20 and if possible, some coins and $1- bills, so that you can pay for bus tickets or food on markets or in restaurants.

Visa and Vaccinations

No visa is required for Ecuador if you want to stay up to 90 days. You only need a valid passport with an empty page for the entry stamp. The passport needs to be valid for 6 months after entering Ecuador. On top of that, you need health insurance that will cover any health issues while you are in Ecuador and a round trip or onward flight ticket. I didn't have an outbound flight ticket, but I flew to the Galapagos and then from the Galapagos to Quito and said I would leave Ecuador by bus. Luckily, I didn't have a problem because of this.

You do need a visa if you are holding a passport of one of the following countries:
Afghanistan, Angola, Bangladesh, Cameroon, Cuba, Democratic People's Republic of Korea (North Korea), Democratic Republic of Congo, Eritrea, Ethiopia, Gambia, Ghana, Guinea, India, Iraq, Kenya, Nepal, Nigeria, Libya, Pakistan, Somalia, Senegal, Sri Lanka, Syria.

Vaccinations

The usual routine vaccinations are recommended for Ecuador. Besides, if you plan on working with animals or if you will spend a longer amount of time in the Amazon, it's recommended to have an anti-rabies vaccination. A yellow fever vaccination is not mandatory since the year 2000. However, you need proof of the yellow fever vaccination if you arrive from a country that is considered to be a yellow fever risk area (for example Brazil or Angola).

There are cases of dengue fever, Malaria, yellow fever, and the zika virus. To prevent these diseases, wear long clothes when mosquitos are active and use an anti-mosquito spray with a high DEET factor. To avert mosquitos, locals gave me the following tip (I haven't tried it but so many people have sworn that this works): Every morning you should put 40 drops of Propolis (Propoleo) in half a cup of water and drink it. Start with this treatment 5 days before you go to a mosquito-infested area.

Climate and the best time to travel

Ecuador's weather changes between dry and wet season. The dry season is between May/June and November and the warmer wet season lasts from December to April/May. However, this doesn't yet tell us what the best time would be to travel. That rather depends on which of the various activities you are interested in that Ecuador has to offer. For the coast, the sky is clearer, and the days are warmer during the wet season. During the dry season, days are often overcast and chilly. On the other hand, whale season coincides with the dry season and if you want to see the spectacle of big humpback whales doing tricks in front of your small boat, you need to visit Ecuador between June and October.

For the highlands and hiking it's more advisable to visit during the dry season. On the other hand, the weather around the volcanos can go through a change of four seasons during any day of the year and therefore you should pack enough layers.

In the Amazon, it rains throughout the whole year but most in December and January, when it could get hard to spot wildlife due to the lush flora or roads could get flooded. At the end of the dry season, the water passages will have dried out and the lodges have to shut down for a month or two. So, the best time to do a trip to the Amazon in Ecuador is April to July.

For the Galapagos, the best time to visit is the warmer time of the year which lasts from December to May. Christmas time, early January and July and August are the peak tourist seasons for the Galapagos (as well as the rest of Ecuador) and prices might be more expensive or accommodations rather full. Therefore, the best months for the Galapagos are probably April and May.

As you see, the best time for a visit depends on what you want to do, and you can have a good trip during the whole year. I've been to Ecuador in August and September and was generally happy with the weather I had. Except for the water temperature on the Galapagos being brain-freezingly cold.

Drinking water

The tap water in Ecuador is not safe to drink for tourists and you could suffer from severe stomach infects if you drink tap water. Therefore, buy water bottles or water bags with filtered water, even if someone will tell you that the water is drinkable (potable). Also with ice cubes, you should always ask whether they are made of filtered water. I went so far that I brushed my teeth with filtered water. Luckily, this way, I had no health problems.
Sometimes, there are water dispensers or water filters in the accommodations, where you can fill up your bottles

free of charge. You recognize the filter tap if, next to the faucet, there is a smaller faucet to which you can divert the water by turning a lever. This is the pipe for filtered water.

In order not to contribute to a lot of plastic waste and to always have a clean source of drinking water available, I use a travel water filter. Usually, you can screw the filter to the top of your water bottle.

Consequently, you can avoid plastic waste, save money, and certainly always have drinking water, even if you arrive at a new place in the middle of the night and the shops are already closed. You can buy a travel water filter in sport shops or travel shops.

How to stay safe in Ecuador

I only once felt slightly unsafe in Ecuador while returning from the bus station to my hostel in the old town of Quito at night. Deserted streets in the historic center of Quito after dark aren't the place to be. Yet, luckily, nothing happened and so, 98% of my stay I spent worry-free. However, I did hear firsthand stories of other tourists who were robbed in Quito or on night buses. In order that this doesn't happen to you, I included a list of 7 tips, how you can avoid getting yourself in a dangerous situation in Ecuador.

- **Ask the locals about safety advice**

Locals know best how safe a certain place is. So, ask your hotel or hostel if you can hike to that waterfall by yourself or if it's okay to take a public bus to a certain place. If in doubt, I contacted my hostels beforehand whether it was safe to reach them by public transport or whether I should take a taxi. You can use Google Translate to translate your questions into Spanish or just see if they speak English.

- **Stay in populated areas**

It's more likely that you get robbed if you are the only person in an alley. Therefore, try to explore the parts of the town where other people are out and about as well. On the other hand, if you are in very crowded areas such as public buses in Quito or anywhere during a festival, don't bring any valuables or never put them out of your hands.

- **Don't wear jewelry**

Perhaps, I overdid this a little, but better safe than sorry. I left my finger ring at home and didn't wear my watch, earrings nor any bracelets or necklaces. The best protection is if you don't present yourself as if you have money or as if you have something that is worth getting stolen.

- **Leave your phone in the hostel locker if you don't absolutely need it**

I took pictures with my phone in all the cities and luckily, I'm still in possession of it. Twice, locals warned me that I should put my phone away as someone might rip it out of my hands (both times this was in the historic part of Quito). However, I just tried to be very much aware of who was around me while using my phone. It's not like someone will steal your phone as soon as you snap a picture. The more alert you are while using your phone, the less it will get stolen. What is dangerous is when you go out at night or are in very crowded places and keep your phone in your pants' pocket or purse. If you can avoid it, don't bring your phone when you go out in the evening or when you go to the beach. Safely zip it somewhere inside your jacket when you are on a night bus or getting on or off a bus.

- **Use Uber or Cabify**

In Quito and Guayaquil Uber and Cabify are available. I found Cabify to be cheaper most of the times. These two taxi-services are trackable which makes them safer. While I used the bus during the day and in the evening, it's not always advisable to walk from the hostel to the bus station or any other short distances after dark. Better order an Uber or let someone else order one for you, in case you didn't bring your phone.

- **Spread your money**

Don't keep all your cards and money in one wallet. Spread them across several places of your luggage. Only always bring as much money as you think you will need for the time you will spend out of the hostel. In Ecuador, it is not yet very common to pay with a credit card (except for big hotels) and, therefore, you will need to take small bills and coins of USD with you. Some people keep a fake wallet with a small amount of money with them, which they can hand over in case they do get robbed.

- **Walk around with a plastic bag or cheap shopping bag**

Instead of an expensive-looking purse or camera bag, just bring your camera or anything else you carry with you in a cheap plastic bag. I traveled through South America with a free, reusable shopping bag and sometimes carried my laptop around in it while nobody would have expected that. Make yourself look like you have nothing worth robbing.

So, with those tips, I hope you will only experience the positive sides of Ecuador.

Covid travel regulations

Because everything changes so quickly regarding Covid, it's necessary that you check the most up to date rules before you book your trip and then again before you start it.
I strongly hope that by the time you are reading this book, Covid won't rule over the travel industry anymore. However, if Covid regulations are still in place, there are three things you need to check:

1. What regulations does Ecuador currently have? Can your nationality enter the country? Do you need proof of a test or a vaccine?
The current requirements for Ecuador can be checked on this website: https://ecuador.travel/en/travel-safe-in-ecuador-2/
At the time of writing this book, people of 3 years and older needed proof of vaccination that was completed at

least 2 weeks in advance or a PCR test that was done less than 72 hours before arriving in Ecuador. In addition, everyone has to fill out an online health form prior to flying on this website:
https://declaracionsalud-viajero.msp.gob.ec/

2. Are there any obligations when returning to your country?
You might need to get an antigen test or a PCR test and perhaps Ecuador is on your countries quarantine list. Testing facilities in Ecuador are available.

3. Do you need a test or vaccine for the airline you are flying with or because of the stopover you are having?
Best contact the airline for information about that if you aren't sure.

How to avoid altitude sickness

Altitude sickness is no joke and can even put you in the hospital. You surely want to avoid a trip to a doctor or feeling lousy during your vacation. Altitude sickness can or can't affect anyone, no matter how fit, unfit, sportive, or lazy they are. It sometimes doesn't make sense who gets hit by it. If you arrive from sea level, you might already get out of breath while walking up a flight of stairs at 2000 m. If you arrive from a more elevated country, let's say from 800 m in Austria, you will probably be fine at that elevation.

Ecuador has several cities that are located at an altitude above 2500 m, for example, Papallacta (3300 m), Tulcán (2980 m), Quito (2850 m), Riobamba (2750 m), Latacunga (2750 m), Ambato (2580 m), and Cuenca (2560 m). Apart from the cities, Ecuador has several high-altitude volcanos where you can go trekking. For example, Chimborazo with an altitude of 6270 m, Cotopaxi (5900 m), Pichincha (4780m) or Quilotoa Lake (3910 m).

For many people, 2500 m is the benchmark where they start feeling minor symptoms of altitude sickness. Unfortunately, some people even suffer gravely from it. Therefore, read the following information and tips carefully and you will hopefully pass your stay in Ecuador without any kind of problems.

Symptoms of altitude sickness

It starts with a dry skin and a dry throat. Any kind of exercise (walking stairs or a hill) will be much harder than it normally is and make you dizzy. Even turning around in bed could give you a racing heart. You could have a headache, and you'll probably feel bloated. If it gets really bad, you will feel sick and throw up. If you get a fever too or this lasts more than two days, see a doctor and try to get to a lower level of elevation. That is the best remedy anyway.

Tips to avoid altitude sickness

1. Stay hydrated

Especially if you arrive by plane, it's important that you drink three liters of water in 24 hours. The dry air on the plane dehydrates you and the high elevation does the same.

2. No alcohol on the first day (or even afterward, if you feel symptoms of altitude sickness)

Alcohol dehydrates you in addition to the dry air and if you feel dizzy already, it's not helpful to infuse your blood with alcohol.

3. Take it easy

Don't climb a mountain after a night bus or after arriving from a place at a lower altitude. Even if you have been above 5000 m before and felt fine, the altitude of 3000 m might affect you the next time, if you descended to sea level in the meantime. So, always relax on your first day at a high altitude. Simply take leisurely walks around town. See how you're doing and then plan excursions for the following days.

4. Eat light

The altitude will squeeze your intestines together like a plastic bottle. Everything that doesn't fit will come out. You'll notice it from the smell on buses that people are farting way more than normal. So, in order not to feel sick, try to pick out the onions in your food on the first day and don't start with a greasy burger and fries. Perhaps stick to soup and something with vegetables.

5. Drink coca tea

This helped me when I was climbing Cotopaxi at 5000 m. Coca leaves give you energy and help if you have an upset stomach or a headache. It also was the one "food" a girl on our Uyuni tour could stomach who felt sick (poor girl).

While it's hard to find coca leaves in common areas of Ecuador, you can easily buy them at high altitude places (for example at the refugio on Cotopaxi).

If you know that you are prone to altitude sickness, you can also buy altitude sickness pills in the pharmacy that contain coca leaves.

With these tips, you can hopefully enjoy trekking, views, and bus rides without feeling sick. Yet, if altitude sickness hits you anyway, perhaps you can find a place that offers oxygen to breathe in. Even better, move to a city lower than 2300 m.

How to have a good experience on Ecuadorian buses

Luckily, Ecuador isn't as big as it's neighboring countries and, therefore, day buses tend to be between 2 and 6 hours long while a night bus might be 10 hours (instead of 15-27 hours in Brazil, Colombia, or Argentina). On the downside, Ecuadorian buses aren't as luxurious as in the other countries. Hence, better bring your own entertainment and snacks.

How to book a ticket

In Ecuador, it's still a bit difficult to enquire about bus times or buy tickets online. Therefore, it's the best and cheapest option to book directly with the bus companies at the bus station. To previously check times and routes, you can search on **Rome2Rio** (https://www.rome2rio.com/). However, usually, there are more options available at the terminal. Your accommodation or a travel agency can help you to purchase bus tickets as well.

How to keep warm on the night bus

Night buses in Ecuador are freezing! I am not kidding about that. I was wearing a hoodie, my down jacket, and my rain jacket. The rain jacket was great to block out the air from the a/c (and the water that was dropping down on me one night – disgusting). Of course, also long pants and socks. Apart from the cold temperatures, night buses in Ecuador have a high rate of tourists who are robbed by pickpockets. Therefore, for Ecuador, my recommendation is to avoid night buses, if possible.

How to stay safe on the bus

I didn't have any problems regarding safety on my bus rides, but I heard several firsthand stories from other tourists who were robbed on buses (day and night) in Ecuador. I always check my big backpack in the compartment below the bus. In that bag, I have my laptop, one of my two credit cards and part of my money. If the bus gets robbed, it's usually on board of the bus by people who come and leave during stops. Therefore, keep anything you take on the bus on your body. The best is if you have an invisible hip belt for your passport, some money, and your phone. Or if you have a pocket with a zipper on your jacket, you can also put the phone in there, while keeping your hand on the pocket. Several phones of other people got stolen while people were sleeping, and they woke up with just their headphone cord in their open pocket. Also, the hand luggage of other people got stolen out of the overhead compartment or from below their seat. Never put your backpack in the upper baggage compartment, even if a supposed bus employee wants to help you store your luggage up there. This, too, is a tactic to steal valuables. Another possibility is that the person sitting behind you can rob you by reaching below the seat. The safest way is to have only clothes, food and water in your hand luggage and to keep this between your legs.

Learn Spanish

For Ecuador, it is very useful if you speak a basic, touristy vocabulary of Spanish. The good news is that you really don't have to know a lot to get by. Yet, it has a big effect on the locals if you utter the first words you say to them in Spanish. They will appreciate your effort and quickly you become friends instead of strangers.

I first started learning Spanish with the free Duolingo app. However, I just didn't make any progress with it as there was so much unnecessary vocabulary that you simply don't need on a trip. Luckily, I then found *busuu*. Or rather, a Russian girl who had been living in Quito for four years recommended it to me. First, you do a test which lets you start learning at exactly your Spanish level (after Duolingo I wasn't a complete beginner anymore) and the way it's set up it makes the words and grammar sink in. I quickly became a fan and bought the premium program to access all the classes. This is a lot cheaper than taking a Spanish course and you can study while being on a plane or bus. I soon could follow conversations between locals. Speaking myself is still hard but it's nice to see that I am making progress every day.

Yet, the best option to learn a language still is to follow a course in the country where the language is spoken. Anywhere in South America, you will be able to find Spanish teachers (for example through your hostel) to have private or small group lessons. So, in case you fall in love with a place, why not spend a few weeks there and practice Spanish? The most popular location to learn Spanish in South America seems to be Montañita. For example: https://www.montanitaspanishschool.com/. The classes are affordable and Montañita is a great beach town that offers many places to party, learn to surf and hang out in hammocks.

Finding your way

As everywhere I go, I used the **maps.me** app on my phone and downloaded Ecuador for offline use. This has been a very useful companion every day and always brought me to the place I wanted to go. You can use it to find points of interest within the city, to get to your accommodation or to follow a hiking route. Tourists can mark spots and write comments and hence you can even discover secret spots which other tourists recommend.

Ecuadorian food and drinks you need to try

While the cuisine of Ecuador is similar to the one of the neighboring countries of Colombia and Peru, I found a few dishes that I couldn't get enough of. The fun part is, that you can find most of those foods at small roadside carts and therefore have a cheap meal. Food quality in Ecuador seems to be good as I never had any stomach problems, no matter whether I ate at a local market, food stand or in a restaurant.

- **Encebollado**

This could be called the national dish of Ecuador as I unfortunately haven't found it in another South American country. People start eating it in the morning after a party night or for lunch. It's a fish stew with lots of onions, lime, cilantro and yuca. Usually, it's served with a package of chifle (fried banana stripes).

At first, I was a bit skeptical how you can eat this first thing in the morning but soon, I could have eaten Encebollado all day long. Actually, my mouth starts watering right now.

- **Ceviche**

While Peru is known to have the best ceviche, I have to say that I liked the ones along the coast of Ecuador just as much. My favorite ceviche I had at the fish market in Puerto Lopez because they also added avocado. Ceviche consists of raw or only quickly braised fish (usually white fish but you can also have it with clams and other type of sea food), lots of lime juice, and cilantro. It is also served with a bowl of chifle but sometimes you have to pay extra for the banana chips.

- **Pan de Yuca**

This turned into my favorite Ecuadorian snack. It was first served to us on the boat on Galapagos after we came back from snorkeling and ever since then I was on a quest to find more pan de yuca.

It's a soft, small bread roll made of yuca flour, butter, and eggs. It is also filled with melted cheese in a perfect balance with the dough and best eaten warm.

- **Llapingachos**

You can find llapingachos as a snack that is sold from roadside carts or as a side along with an almuerzo plate. It's a fried potato pattie that is stuffed with cheese.

- **Tigrillo**

This is an Ecuadorian dish which people have for breakfast. It consists of cooked and mashed plantains with cheese and a fried egg, all mixed. With the right spices, this is incredibly delicious.

- **Cheap lunch menus**

Like most countries in South America, Ecuador also offers good value lunch menus. They are called "almuerzo" and usually include potato soup as a starter, and meat with rice, patacones, yuca or fries as a main dish.

Wi-Fi

All of our accommodations offered free Wi-Fi and once in a while we also found a restaurant and café with Wi-Fi (there is no Starbucks yet and hardly any Mc Donald's). So, to always be able to have an internet connection, you could buy a vacation data package with your phone provider from home, or you buy a local SIM card after arriving. *Claro* and *Movistar* are the biggest providers and offer good data plans. So, simply visit one of their shops after arriving and exchange your SIM-card through a local one. Keep your own SIM card in a safe place meanwhile, that you can insert it again when you go home.

How to pick your accommodation

Since travelers all have their individual preferences about what standard their accommodation needs to be, I hardly include recommendations for hostels or hotels. The best deals for Ecuador you get by booking all your accommodations on **booking.com** and reaching genius level. There, you also have all the latest reviews for the hostels and can get an opinion about a place before getting there. If you want a more local experience, you should look for gems on **Airbnb.com**.

Usually, I only book one night and if I like the place, I extend my stay. Of course, this doesn't work during local holidays and other special occasions.

Tips how to find cheap flights to Ecuador (and to any other country for that matter)

If you think that flights from Europe to South America are expensive, check for flight prices from one country in South America to another. It's just as much if not more! Yet, if you know how to search, you can find good deals to fly to Quito. Try to book with the following tips to find a cheap plane ticket for yourself.

1 Use several flight search engines

I usually start looking for flights on **Skyscanner.net** and then I compare the deals from there with **CheapTickets** and/or **Opodo**. These sites tend to have the cheapest prices. Skyscanner for example, lets you set a price alert which will inform you with an e-mail when they have cheaper flights. You could do that half a year before your trip. Another possibility is to type your flight into Google directly to get an estimate of how much the airfare will be. In the end, I always check on the websites of my favorite airlines directly. For South America, they are Swiss and LATAM.

2 Be early and buy your flight at least 3 months in advance

If you know the dates of your vacation, there is no use to wait with booking your flights. They will only get more expensive.

On the other hand: In times of covid, you should plan all your travel last-minute. Once you are sure that the country you want to visit is open and it will be agreeable to travel under the current circumstances.

3 Be slightly flexible

Check the dates three days prior and after the dates you chose to fly. There might be a difference up to $300! If you search with CheapTickets or Skyscanner it's very easy to have an overview of the flight prices at different dates.

4 Travel from other airports and book multi-leg flights

Especially if you travel from Europe, it makes sense to check the airports in the surrounding countries and then buying a connecting flight from your country to get there. Cheaper airports to fly from are Barcelona, London, Frankfurt am Main, Düsseldorf, Paris, Milan, Amsterdam, and Brussels. So, yes, if you have enough time, it's sometimes worth it to travel in several legs. If you fly from the US, often Miami and LAX are the cheapest. Just calculate enough time in your connecting airport in case your first plane is delayed because you will have to go get your luggage and check it in for your new flight.

However: In times of covid, you should opt for a direct flight, since every additional stop can mean more tests, more regulations, and a possible quarantine.

5 Delete your browser history

The websites where you searched for your flight tickets to Ecuador will recognize you on your second visit and raise the prices a little since you are still interested. So, if you notice an increase in the price, the first thing to do is to close the website, clear the browser history and then start searching again, once you are ready to book.

6 Sign up for the newsletter from your favorite airlines

Newsletters still offer good value and often you find cheap airfares in them. At the moment, I regularly receive special offers from TUI and Iberia. By the way, **SwissMissOnTour** offers a newsletter as well. Sign up to receive my latest blog posts and a free and helpful packing list.

7 Flying cheap within Ecuador

Since the distances within Ecuador aren't that huge, it didn't make sense for me to fly within the country. However, be aware that all the flights to and from the Galapagos will land in Guayaquil. So, even if you fly to or from Quito, you will have a stop there (which wasn't indicated on my ticket). Further, flights to Lago Agrio (to get to the Amazon in Ecuador) often are delayed a lot and you might miss part of your rainforest tour if you come by plane.

Two-week itinerary to see the best of culture and nature

We will concentrate on mainland Ecuador as this has so much to offer to easily fill two to three weeks. If you also want to visit the Galapagos, you should plan an additional 7-10 days for those islands.

Day 1: Arrival in Quito

After enjoying a spectacular landing at the modern airport of Quito which is surrounded by high, snow-covered mountains and volcanos, you should take it easy to get used to the altitude. Stroll around the historic center and look at some churches and other interesting buildings.

Day 2: Quito and journey to Mindo

Take a half-day trip to *Mitad del Mundo* or stroll around the historical center and climb the tower of the Basilica. At around 4 p.m. you take a bus from La Ofelia to arrive in the green cloud forest of Mindo two hours later. Use the evening to have a delicious meal in town and already spot hummingbirds at your accommodation.

Day 3: Mindo and transfer back to Quito

Get up early to join a bird watching tour or walk toward the Tarabita cable car on your own while trying to spot toucans and other colorful birds. Hike to as many waterfalls as you enjoy before returning back to town. In case you still have time, visit one of the chocolate factories and do a chocolate tasting. At 5 p.m. you take the bus back to Quito.

Day 4: Quito

By now, you should have adapted to the high altitude and a flight of stairs shouldn't get you out of breath anymore. Time to cross the 4000 m line. Take the Teleferico cable car up to Cruz Loma. Walk to the viewpoints from where you have a breath-taking view over Quito (one of the best city views in South America!), take a horseback ride (see the picture on page 38) or even hike the 5-hour loop hike toward Pichincha volcano.
Back in town, you can have dinner and drinks in the Mariscal area or visit the remaining sights you want to see downtown.

Day 5: Latacunga and Quilotoa

Take an early morning bus to Latacunga. Bring your luggage to your accommodation and then return to the bus terminal to take a bus to the Quilotoa Lagoon around lunch time. Enjoy the view across the emerald lagoon or hike down to the water. Book a tour to visit the glacier of Cotopaxi the next day (if you enjoy hiking and feel physically fit).

Day 6: Cotopaxi

Today, you will need a lot of energy as you'll hike up to an altitude of above 5000 meters. The views of the brown volcano with the white peak are spectacular and you will feel a great satisfaction after having achieved this challenging hike. The strong winds don't make it any easier. For this hike, it's necessary to wear proper hiking boots. You can also rent them in Latacunga.

Quilotoa Lagoon

Day 7: Baños

Again, you want to have an early start in order to get to Baños by bus. Drop your bags off at your hostel after the arrival and then dive into your preferred activity for the rest of the day. This could be a hike up to the tree-house swing or an afternoon Chiva tour to the waterfalls. Of course, you should also go soak in one of the hot springs.

Day 8: Baños and bus to Cuenca

The bus drive to Cuenca will take about 7 hours and depending on your preferences, you could spend the complete day in Baños and then take a night bus to Cuenca, where you will arrive before 6 a.m.
If you don't like night buses, you have to leave Baños before noon, as most hostels in Cuenca only allow check-in until 9 p.m. Be sure to book a bus that drives directly to Cuenca without heading up to Quito first.

Day 9: Cuenca

Get up early today (or simply drop your bags off at the hostel after the night bus) and head to Cajas National Park for a half-day trip. Marvel at the stunning marshland with black lakes and green mountain peaks. In the evening, go and relax at one of the luxurious but affordable spas.

Day 10: Cuenca and drive to Montañita

The morning you spend strolling around the city center of Cuenca. Browse through the artisanal markets and check out some of the free museums. Have a delicious lunch and fruit juice at one of the markets. At around 2 p.m. you should take a bus to Montañita via Guayaquil. In case you want to visit the Galapagos, this would be a good moment to start the trip, as all flights to the Galapagos depart and land in Guayaquil.

If you don't travel to the Galapagos, you will arrive in Montañita in the evening. If it's any night from Wednesday to Saturday, you can get a taste of Montañita's party life.

Day 11: Montañita

Enjoy the beach and perhaps hit the waves with a surfboard. Be sure to eat a ceviche or encebollado at the beach.

Day 12: Montañita

Spend another day at the beach or relaxing in a hammock. You could also hike to one of the viewpoints along the shore.

Day 13: Puerto Lopez

In case you are here between June and October, book a whale watching trip for today in Puerto Lopez. The transport from Montañita is included in the price. Bring all your luggage and leave it at the travel agency as you will travel on to Quito later in the day (you won't return to Montañita).

The bus trip to Quito takes about 9 hours. You could leave past lunchtime and arrive in Quito late in the evening, where you take an Uber to your hostel, or you take a night bus from Puerto Lopez in the evening and spend the day at the beach. This really depends on whether you like night buses and at what time you have your return flight the next day. Don't take any risks of missing the flight.

Day 14: Quito and return flight

Unfortunately, your adventure in Ecuador is already over and your heart and camera will be filled with many happy memories of this diverse country. Perhaps, you have time to visit one more church or museum in Quito and can eat one more cheap lunch at the central market before boarding your plane back home or onward.

Now, let's have a closer look at the individual places.

Quito

Quito calls itself the center of the world and with its location on the Equator, this might be rightful. It's a big city with a beautiful historic center. The town lies on 2300 m and is surrounded by several higher mountains and volcanoes, offering splendid views. If you land in Quito or fly out of here, get a window seat. You're in for a treat.

Since Quito is quite elevated, you might get out of breath very easily after arriving, especially if you came from sea level. So, take it easy for the first two days and don't visit a volcano or the Teleferico right away. Drink lots of water and you will get accustomed to the altitude within 36 hours.

How to get from the airport to the city center

Official taxis to the historic center cost $28. Uber is available too and costs about the same.

The cheapest way is to take a public bus for $2 to the central terminal. Then, you could take a taxi from there ($2 or $3 depending on where you go). Or another bus for $0.25. The bus journey takes about 50 minutes and the taxi from the airport to the hotel would take 30 to 40 minutes.

As I waited for the bus, many taxi drivers approached me and, in the end, I shared the taxi with a local. He paid $5 and I paid $10 and they brought me directly to my hostel. So, if you speak some Spanish and have some patience for haggling, you should get the taxi down to $15 if you are by yourself.

Arriving in Quito by bus

Quito has two big bus stations. Quitumbe for southern departures and Carcelen for northern departures. Both can be reached by public bus. You can check your route on Google Maps. Usually, it takes at least 30 minutes or up to one hour to reach a bus terminal with public transport from the touristic areas. Hence, you might want to take a taxi to get to or from the bus station.

What to do in Quito

There is a lot to do in the different neighborhoods of Quito and in its surroundings. You can easily spend 4 or 5 nights in Quito.

Walk around the historic center

Quito seems to have a nice church or a colorful colonial-style building at every street corner. A must-see is the church of *La Compañía de Jesús* with its golden interior.

Climb the towers of the Basilica

You will see the majestic basilica towering over Quito from many locations. Make your way here and then pay $2 to climb the towers and enjoy the views. This is both thrilling and nice because of the architecture.

Stand on the northern and southern hemisphere at the same time

Participate in a day tour for $10 which brings you to a viewpoint for Pichincha volcano and after that to the sights area of *Mitad del Mundo*. There are many small museums and entertaining activities concerning gravity within the area of Mitad del Mundo.

If you visit Mitad del Mundo on your own, you can take a taxi for about $8. Or you take a public bus to *La Ofelia* bus station and then the connection to Mitad del Mundo for 40 cents in total. The entry fee to the monument and all the other activities is $5.

Indulge yourself in chocolate

Ecuador is a big cacao producer and in Quito, you can try local products at the *Pacari* shops or at *Republica de Chocolate* (both near Plaza Grande). Of course, you can drink delicious hot or cold chocolate in all the cafés (ask if its local and "no es polvo"). You don't want to drink powder chocolate from the supermarket after all.

Ride the Teleferico (cable car) and enjoy the view

It has never been easier to get to 4000 m and have an amazing view.

Take a taxi for $3 from the historic center to get to the station for the cable car. There is no bus station near the cable car entrance and since it's on a steep hill, it's worth it to take the taxi.

47

At the foot of the mountain, there also is a small amusement park with rides for kids.

The round-trip ride with the Teleferico costs $8.50 and each way takes 9 minutes. The views from the cable car are stunning already as you begin to realize how big Quito really is.

At the top, you could do a 4–5-hour loop hike to Pichincha volcano. Bring a windbreaker jacket and something to cover your head and ears. The average temperature is 6 degrees, however, if it's not cloudy, the sun is still very strong. Don't forget to put on sunscreen!

Even if you don't do the loop hike, walk uphill to the right for 10 minutes to reach a platform with swings. Get your awesome Instagram pictures and marvel at the incredible view. From there, walk another 5 minutes to get to the next platform. A little to the back, you will now see a pasture with horses.

Either do a 45-minutes horseback ride for $10 or take some deep breaths and hike up the very steep hill right in front of you. That's as far as you need to go for the best views in case you don't want to do the complete loop.

We did the horseback ride and absolutely loved it! Tranquility, magnificent views, and we even received a poncho during the ride to feel like locals.

Visit a museum

Quito has more than 50 museums and a lot of them are free. My two favorite ones are:

- **Centro Cultural Metropolitano (CCMQ)**

This museum pulls in visitors with interesting exhibitions that change regularly. Since it's located right in front of the presidential palace and is free to visit, it is really worth checking it out.

Address: Garcia Moreno 887 and Espejo, closed on Mondays.

- **Centro de Arte Contemporaneo (CAC)**

This museum is free as well and already the architecture of the building is nice to have a look at. The exhibitions change frequently and since it's modern art, you sometimes find treasures and sometimes don't understand what exactly you are looking at.
Apart from the art exhibitions there also are many music and theater events at the CAC.

Address: Montevideo and Luis Davila. Closed on Mondays.

Dance Salsa or Bachata

I dance Salsa in Switzerland, so for me, Quito and Ecuador in general are like paradise. All day long you hear Salsa music coming out of restaurants and cafes and on the buses as well.

Many hostels offer free Salsa lessons, but Quito would also be a good place to take a few private lessons.
Go out in the evening. Even if you don't dance yourself, it's amazing to watch the pro dancers feel the rhythms. For example, **Salsoteca Lavoe** (www.salsotecalavoe.com/) has Salsa parties on several nights during the week. On my first visit, I got there at 9 p.m. on a Tuesday and it was very easy to find someone to dance with and then being asked to other dances.

On Friday, there was live music, and the awesome thing is that there were about 20 taxi dancers. They were especially there to dance with people who are there without a partner.

You can also easily go to Lavoe by bus (*Estadio* station). There are direct buses from the historic center (Troley Q, see on Google Maps).

Where to stay in Quito

I loved my stay at **Masaya Hostel**. That was probably the nicest hostel I ever stayed at, with spacious, comfy dorm beds that offered privacy. Plus, Masaya offers free activities every day like yoga and dance classes or chocolate tasting.

However, the hostel is located in the historic center. During the day, there is a lot to see and do, however, after sunset, the area is deserted. Therefore, it might be more fun for you to stay in the Mariscal area. There, I stayed at the **Selina**, which was well located, however, it wasn't clean.

One thing you need to do in the Mariscal area in case you like Mexican food is eating at *Lucha Libre* Mexican restaurant. They offer cheap lunch menus, and the food was very tasty.

Day trips from Quito

If you are short on time, you can do the following trips as day trips from Quito. For Quilotoa and Cotopaxi I recommend spending a few days in that region to get accustomed to the altitude.

Visit the Otavalo Market

On Saturdays and Wednesdays, Otavalo hosts the biggest arts & crafts market in the country, if not South America. Find colorful souvenirs like bags, ponchos, and paintings.

I liked the market, but it wasn't worth the two-hour journey, especially if you have seen other markets in Peru or Bolivia.

You can get to Otavalo by taking a taxi ($8, 30 minutes) from the tourist center in Quito to **Carcelen** bus station. Or take a bus (via Ofelia bus station for $0.25, 50 minutes). From there, buses to Otavalo depart every 10 minutes. The journey takes 2 hours and leads past impressive valleys and green hills. It's a very picturesque ride on a comfortable coach bus and of course, there is Salsa music during the journey.

Climb to the glacier of Cotopaxi

For $50 you can book an organized day trip to the glacier of the picturesque Cotopaxi volcano. Some tours even offer an adventurous bike ride down the mountain. This is a good tour option if you are short on time. The same goes for Quilotoa Lagoon. Tours can easily be booked at hostels in Quito.

If you have more time, read the chapter about **Latacunga** and the sights in that area.

Marvel at Lagoa de Quilotoa

Another day trip to the Cotopaxi region is to the stunningly green Quilotoa Lagoon. This day trip you can do by public transport if you get up early and take the bus to Latacunga for $2.50/2hrs and then to the lagoon, another $2.50 and two hours. However, it's more relaxed if you can spend a night or two in the Latacunga region.

Mindo

This small town two hours out of Quito welcomes you with a relaxed vibe, waterfalls, and lots of nice hostels with green spaces to watch birds like hummingbirds and toucans. If that's too boring for you, go on a night walk and discover snakes, frogs, and spiders.

How to get to Mindo

Go to La Ofelia bus station in Quito. The buses leave from the terminal next to it. Just ask an employee or a police officer in case you are unsure where to go. Bus times are 8 a.m., 9 a.m., 11 a.m., 1 p.m., and 4 p.m.
One-way costs $3.10 and the journey takes two hours on a coach bus.

What to do in Mindo

Mindo is a paradise for bird watchers, chocolate and meat lovers.

Taste local chocolate

There are three places where you can have a chocolate tour. I have visited chocolate factories in Switzerland and have to say that the tours in my country are better, and the chocolate is sweeter. In Mindo, you only find dark chocolate with hardly any sugar. So, chocolate that's actually good for your health. However, small bars start at $5, which I find quite expensive.

I had breakfast and a hot chocolate at *Mindo Chocolate*. The pancakes were good, with lots of fruit, however, the chocolate tasted like Ovomaltine (a taste I hate) and therefore, I didn't try any other product of theirs although their chocolate tour is the cheapest at $6.

Then, there is *Yumbo Chocolate*. You can taste their chocolate in the shop (so, you don't really need a tour for $8). I had a brownie for $2.50 which was divine!! Best brownie ever.

Then, I did the tour at *Queztal Chocolate* for $10. Compared to the others, they have an actual chocolate production site apart from the restaurant. We got to eat the cacao fruit and taste the beans and nibs and visited every step of the process from the trees to fermentation to packaging. If you come to Switzerland, there are great displays to have a similar experience. The only thing you can't have in Switzerland is a visit of the cacao trees in the garden. However, if you haven't yet been to a chocolate factory, this tour will be very entertaining for you.

At the end, we could taste all of their chocolates (which you also can in the shop for free), received a chocolate tea and a piece of brownie (which also was divine!)

So, just for the brownies, a trip to Mindo will be worth it :)

Go bird watching

If you are a bird lover, you should join a guided morning walk which will cost between $50 and $75. If you like birds but don't want to pay so much, you still get to see a lot of them by just walking around the forest or to the Tarabita cable car. Plus, most hostels feed the hummingbirds. You can see them everywhere and there are so many colorful species! I enjoyed watching them and the other birds although I am not usually that into birds.

Do a night walk

Night walks start at 7 p.m. and cost $15 for about 1.5 hours. I didn't do one because I hate spiders and if you go on a night walk you will see them the size of your palm and bigger. You will also see snakes and cute tree frogs. The people who joined the walks were all really happy that they did.

Hike to six waterfalls

From town, you need to get to the Tarabita cable car. It's a 1.5-hour uphill walk or a $6 taxi ride. You will walk on the main road, but you can still have nice views of the surrounding mountains. Plus, if you go between 6.30 and 8.30 in the morning you have a good chance of spotting toucans. I was lucky enough to spot two of them. Before seeing them, I heard them as they have the loudest cries! I also saw some hummingbirds and squirrels along the way and of course butterflies.

About the Tarabita

The Tarabita is a yellow "basket" made of metal that will bring you across the valley. You can choose to ride each way or walk one way (25 minutes and you'll pass Cascada Nambillo) or both ways. Either way, you have to pay $5 to get access to the area, which you can pay at the entrance of the Tarabita.

The waterfalls

As I have seen many waterfalls, those weren't that special to me. However, I liked Cascada Ondinas and Cascada Guarumos the best. I also took a nicely refreshing bath at Guarumos waterfall. You can reach them in 30 and 35 minutes from the other end of the Tarabita.

On the way back, I walked past the taxis on the parking lot and thought I would perhaps catch a cheaper taxi along the way. However, I was even luckier because the guy who rode the Tarabita with me stopped and gave me a ride. It turned out that he was the owner of the Tarabita, which his dad had built 17 years ago. They bought the whole mountain (including the waterfalls). So, in case you want to buy a mountain, come look for one in Ecuador :D

Where to eat in Mindo

Apart from the chocolate and brownies, Mindo had other culinary highlights.

Eat steak (lomo) from the hot stone at *El Chef*. They will cook it (or quickly drop it in the pan) to your delight and it's marinated in a garlic sauce. Extremely delicious! It's a big portion of meat and comes with not so crunchy fries and a good vegetable salad. All this for $9.80. You can't say no. They also offer non-steak almuerzos for $3.50.

Then, I had the best fried chicken and fries with garlic sauce (or ketchup and mayo) for $1.50 at *Asadero "los parceros" y salchipapas*. They are located at the down right corner of Mindo park, a little bit into the street on the right side. Since food in Mindo is a bit more expensive than in other cities in Ecuador, this came as a surprise treat.

Where to stay in Mindo

I stayed at Cinnamon House which was clean and had comfortable dorm beds with curtains. I loved the outdoor area with the many hanging chairs and the place to watch hummingbirds.

Baños (de Agua Santa)

If you go to Baños, make sure that you travel during daylight hours as the landscape during the bus ride is simply stunning. Set in green mountains with a river cutting through the valley and a lot of waterfalls jumping over cliffs, Baños is a good place to go and take some deep breaths and enjoy a local coffee or hot chocolate.

How to get to Baños

There are almost hourly buses from Quito (Quitumbe, 3 hours, $4), Latacunga (1.5 hours $2.50), and Cuenca (7 hours, $11).

From Montañita there is an option to take a night bus via Santa Elena as the journey time is shorter. However, since the scenery is breathtaking, I took the route along the coast via Guayaquil. Montañita to Guayaquil takes 3 hours ($6) and buses depart hourly.

From Guayaquil to Baños, the journey takes 6 to 7 hours ($10.25) and it's a very windy road (but beautiful). From Guayaquil there are three buses (7 a.m. / 10.45 a.m. / 12.40 p.m.) plus some night buses between 9 and 11 p.m.

What to do in Baños

Baños offers a lot of adventure activities if you are prepared to spend some money. To relax, you then can soak in the hot springs after the activities.

Visit the waterfalls

Now, even if you are not a huge fan of waterfalls, Pailón del Diablo (cost: $2) will impress you. The visitor's path is awesome as it leads over suspension bridges and behind, on top of, below and along the waterfall. You can inspect the full power of Pailón del Diablo from all sides.

The other waterfalls along the *ruta de las cascadas* are okay but not very special. Yet, it's a worthwhile journey as the valley is simply stunning.

There are two ways to visit the waterfalls. By tourist bus or by mountain bike.

1) Visit Pailon del Diabolo on a Chiva Tour

Chivas are open tourist trucks that play loud reggaeton music. If you choose this method, you will probably be the only foreign tourist among many Ecuadorians. Yet, I had a great time on the party bus! You can book Chiva tours at any tour office in town for $3 to $4 for 3 hours. They depart every three hours (10.30/1.30/4.30).
The downside is that you will stop at touristy places where people can pay to do ziplines or ride the tarabita and you won't stop to look at the other waterfalls along the way. But you see them from the truck (sit on the right side).

Also, there are two entrances to Pailón del Diablo, and you only enter at the first one (from the top). It's amazing and a good way to see the waterfall. So, if you just want a local, fun and comfortable excursion, take a Chiva.

If you want to see it from the other entrance too, you could still go back the next day by bicycle.

2) Bike ride toward Puyo

You can rent a bike at the tour offices in town for $6. Check them out first and see if the quality and height is to your liking. Bring a rain jacket as rain can start suddenly and torrential in Baños. The road then becomes slippery and staying out of the way of broad cars and trucks that use the same path is even more difficult. These are the downsides of the bike ride. The upsides are that it's downhill or flat and that you can stop wherever you want. There are many stunning spots and waterfalls (7!) where you will want to take pictures. You can ride past the adventure parks, or you can choose to do ziplines if you feel like it. Also, at Pailón del Diablo you can visit both sides.

Then, you can ride along the road to Puyo for however long you enjoy the landscape and when you want to head back to Baños, stop at a bus stop. Buses will bring you and your bike back to Baños for $2. Just calculate some time until a bus can take you. The first two buses that drove past us were full and we had to wait quite a while.

Go river rafting or canyoning

I didn't do this as it was between 3 and 10 °C while I was in Baños, however, it's a common thing to do and you can book it in many tour offices.

Swing high above the city at Casa del Arbol

If you haven't been on the (free) swings at the Teleferico in Quito, head up this mountain (2.5 hrs. by walking or a 30-minute bus/chiva ride for $2.50). You get great views over the beautiful scenery and can enjoy it while swinging from a tree house. The entrance to the tree house costs $1 and about another dollar for each swing you want to use.

Experience a hot spring

I say experience as it's something you should do while you are in South America, but you will be disappointed if you expect a nice clean Spa. We heard that the hot springs in town are very crowded and therefore headed to **Termas el Salado** (entrance fee: $3/ taxi ride for $2 or a 20-minutes' walk). However, there only was one hot pool, and the other ones were lukewarm and so the hot pool was very crowded. The watercolor of the pools is a muddy brown. Perhaps you can have a more relaxing experience with less people in the morning. We went at 5 p.m.
The cool thing is that you can go down to the river from the pool and cool down below a natural waterfall.

Experience a massage

You can have a full body massage with hot stones and a facial mask for $15 to $25 per hour. While my massage was a bit hard and therefore not very relaxing, I did enjoy the warmth of the hot stones and the mask made of Amazonian chocolate. So, the whole experience was worthwhile.

Eat at mercado central

The central market is open from the early morning to 6 p.m. You can have local meals like hornado (meat from an entire pig) or encebollado starting at $2.50.

Relax in a café

There are many cafés in Baños with a big selection, good coffee, and good prices (no international chains).

Where to stay

I stayed at **Papachos** which was a 5 min walk from the center of town. The beds had good mattresses and curtains. The hostel was clean and had a good vibe. Ask for a second blanket (una colcha) if it's cold.

Latacunga

Latacunga is the gateway to a beautiful hiking area. You can start tours to Cotopaxi volcano (which you have probably seen from the plane) or embark on the 3 to 5-day Quilotoa loop hike.

Latacunga itself is small and easy to navigate. It offers a nice park with palm trees and enough different restaurants to fill the belly of a tourist.

How to get to Latacunga

From Baños:

You take a bus for $2.50 for about 1.5 hours. Buses leave almost every 30 minutes. They will drop you off at a big intersection along the highway. There you wait for the next bus that passes into town or hop on a colectivo taxi to the central bus station. This costs $0.50.

From or to Quito:

Buses leave hourly from the central bus station in Latacunga and take 2 hours for $2.50. If you depart from Quito, you have to board a bus at terminal Quitumbe.

What to do around Latacunga

As I said, it's a great place to set out for day hikes or multi-day hikes. However, the most important is that you acclimatize yourself properly to the altitude before you start any hikes. Spend at least 3 days in a city above 2000m (Quito or Latacunga) before you attempt any hikes. If you arrive freshly off the plane from Europe or a place by the sea, your heart will pump wildly just by going up a flight of stairs at this altitude. However, if you give your body some days to adjust and perhaps drink some relaxing coca tea, you should be fine on the walk to the glacier of Cotopaxi at 5100 m.

Hike Cotopaxi

This has been one of the highlights of my trip! Cotopaxi's beauty is comparable to that of mount Fuji in Japan. It offers incredible views with its snow-covered top and brownish, desert-like base. It's almost 6000 m high and experienced mountain climbers can book multi-day tours to the crater.

I am not a big fan of hiking, but I enjoy it from time to time. So, I am not the fittest hiker but with proper acclimatization and one small step after the other I managed to get up to the glacier at 5100m. If you want to do the same, I recommend booking a tour with transport, a guide, and lunch. I paid $35 and booked it through my hostel (*Old House Backpackers*). Probably, you could get it for $30 but mine included hiking boots as well, which I could use the day before, so that my feet could get used to them.

Pick-up was at 8.30 a.m. and the ride to the park took about an hour. Just as we arrived, the clouds cleared away and we saw the whole mountain majestically towering in front of us. Luckily, it stayed like that during the entire hike. Our guide was very surprised as a usual day at Cotopaxi is partly to mostly cloudy and incredibly windy (bring a windbreaker jacket, hat, and scarf! Also, put on sunscreen as the sun is stronger up here.). However, we were blessed with only a little wind and no clouds. I hope the same for your visit.

We reached the parking lot at 4500 m at 10 a.m. and started the hike along a serpentine ascent. It's very sandy and you absolutely need hiking boots with a good grip that go above your ankles.
Even here, we felt the altitude and it was crucial that everyone in the group walked at their own speed. If you walk baby steps in slow motion (like I did), you will reach the refuge hut in 1 hour.

There, you take a break and eat the snacks you brought or buy a warm coca tea for $2.50. Once you caught your breath you can continue for another 45 minutes to get below the glacier. Some years ago, it was possible to actually hike to the glacier and touch it. However, now the guides advise against it. They will bring you to a stop sign 100 m below the glacier (where the glacier used to be). We saw some people climb the last 100 m anyway, but the guides were not happy as it's a lot steeper here and the danger of big rocks rolling on top of you is very high.

So, on a day with a bad view, it's perhaps not worth it to climb past the refuge hut. But on a day with a good view, it is awesome to approach the summit just a little closer and have a view down a different side of the mountain. Just watch every step you take as it is steeper past the refuge hut! Even when you go down. The return path below the refuge hut was way easier as you could kind of float down on the loose sand. However, I probably wouldn't have found that good path by myself and was glad that we had a guide.

By 1.30 p.m. we had our lunch in a restaurant in a lower part of the national park. After that, we quickly visited a lagoon which wasn't special compared to Quilotoa lagoon and there, it was so windy that it was hard to stand straight.

We were back in Latacunga shortly past 3.30 p.m.

A one-day hike to Quilotoa Lagoon

To get to the lagoon, take a bus from the bus station in Latacunga for $3 to Puerta de Quilotoa. Ask for a seat on the right side of the bus for the good valley views.
It will drop you off at a gate 200 m from the crater of the lagoon. The buses by *Andes Transit* leave at 7 a.m. and 12

noon and take a little over 2 hours but there are also other bus companies.

If you only want to take some pictures of the beautiful lagoon, you will have seen it in 30 minutes. There are some restaurants and even hotels or hostels up there. However, it's usually very windy and not very agreeable to sit outside.

You could also opt to hike down to the lake which will take about 45 minutes and back up one hour.

The return bus leaves from one street up higher than the entry gate where you got off. The bus will be parked along the road for about 20 minutes before it leaves. Ask about the correct return times at the bus station in Latacunga before you leave. My bus left at 4.30 p.m.
Again, it costs $3 and takes 2 hours to Latacunga.

Hiking the Quilotoa Loop

The Quilotoa Loop is a hike for which you will need 3 to 5 days. You will see green hills, blue-green streams, smiling children (bring some candy for them or teach them a game), and lamas. As a reward, you have a stunning view of the Quilotoa Lagoon at the end. However, since you have direct access to the viewing platform of the lagoon from the bus stop, you don't necessarily need to strain yourself with a five-day hike before seeing the lagoon. This hike is more about really being in Ecuador's countryside, meeting new people and following your thoughts while getting lost and having to find the right track again. The nights you will spend in hostels in tiny villages along the way and therefore, you only need to bring a small backpack with water, snacks, clothes, and toiletries. Usually, dinners are included in the price of the hostel. The rest of your things, you should store in your accommodation in Latacunga. Check beforehand if your hostel offers this for free.

Wear proper hiking clothes (hiking boots, poles, and quick-dry clothes) as this will make the strenuous climbs and descends much easier. There are many climbs and descends you will have to achieve and at an altitude of around 3900 m, this isn't a walk in a park.

The typical route is Latacunga -> Sigchos -> Isinlivi -> Chugchilan -> Quilotoa -> Latacunga. Be sure to properly inform yourself about the route in Latacunga before you start in order to minimize the chance of getting lost. Bring enough cash (you can't pay with credit card along the way and there are no ATMs) in case you take a bus or hire a llama along the way to skip part of the hike.

Cuenca

In this city, you find pretty colonial architecture as well as stylish, modern houses. A lot of them are constructed in red brick and so you see a sea of red if you walk to a lookout point. Numerous inviting parks with benches and cool playgrounds are waiting to be discovered as well as beautiful thermal baths and local food markets. Cuenca definitely is a city worth stopping at.

How to get to Cuenca

From Quito (Terminal Quitumbe) or Baños, you have regular buses to Cuenca. The ride takes about 7 hours and 30 minutes from each city and costs around 11 USD. From

Guayaquil, the ride takes about 3.5 hours and costs about 7 USD. Check the website *Rome2Rio* for times.

In case you are coming from Mancora in Peru, Cuenca is a good option to arrive in Ecuador. There are direct night buses from Peru to Cuenca and vice versa.

What to do in Cuenca

When I arrived, I was welcomed with a torrential downpour so that all my things were soaked. Plus, it's kind of difficult to find a restaurant or hostel past 9 p.m. as everything shuts down (so be aware of that with your arrival time). Still, the city managed to enchant me completely.

Visit a free art museum

There are several art museums, and all are free. I particularly liked the **museum of modern art** (there, a donation was appreciated). It was primarily hosting an artist that painted Lego figures in different scenes.

Address: Mariscal Sucre 1527 and Coronel Tálbot, Cuenca.

Opening hours: Monday to Friday from 9 a.m. to 4.45 p.m. Saturday and Sunday: 9 a.m. to 2 p.m.

The **Panama Hat museum** was also good for a quick visit. However, it's more of a shop with very expensive hats with a few hat producing machines to look at.

Address: Calle Larga 10-41. Open from 8.00 a.m. to 12.30 p.m. and 2.30 – 5.30. On Saturday from 8.30 a.m. to 12.30 p.m.

If you like ancient jewelry, ruins, and lamas you should go to the **Pumapungo ruins**. They are located within the city of Cuenca, and you can walk there from the center. It's a museum as well as an outdoor park with animals. Like the other museums, it's free to enter.

Address: Calle Larga and Huayna Capac Esquina. Closed on Mondays. Tue – Fri: 8 a.m. – 5 p.m. and Saturday/Sunday: 10 a.m. to 4 p.m.

Soak in a beautiful thermal spa complex

Agua de Piedra (https://piedradeagua.com.ec/) was the best thermal spa experience I've had! Check out their website as they often offer a 2 for 1 deal. The normal price is $35, and the circuit includes a steam sauna, two hot mud pools, a hot and a cold pool in a cave lit by candles, a steam box, and a warm relaxation pool.

A taxi with a taxi meter from downtown Cuenca is between $4.50 and $5.50.

Enjoy the view from Turi lookout

In my opinion, this view could be skipped if you are short on time, but it still gives you a nice view of the city in red bricks. Take a bus from the corner of 12 de Abril and Solano to get there and back as you otherwise somehow have to find your way around a steep forest area (for example past the Mall of Rio, which is quite a detour). You need a card for the bus though but if you ask some locals, you could give them the 25 cents so that they can pay for you.

In case this sounds too complicated, ask your accommodation if there is a bus stop with a bus to Turi that is closer to your hostel or join the hop on hop off bus for 8 USD which will drive you to many important sights in the city.

Stroll along the river and relax in the parks and squares

Cuenca is an awesome city to simply stroll around as there are many inviting outdoor places and squares with handicraft markets. Especially the walk along the river is picturesque and the park at the planetarium (Parque de la Madre) has a nice playground.

Eat at El Santo

This Mexican restaurant offers such delicious tacos and quesadillas at very reasonable prices that I went back twice.

A half-day trip from Cuenca - visit Cajas National Park

I almost made the mistake of skipping this national park but it's so stunningly beautiful that you could cry. This area of green hills and black lakes is a must and on top, it's very easy to get there.

Catch an *Occidental* bus from the Terminal Terrestre to the entrance of Cajas National Park. There is about one bus every hour between 8 a.m. and 4 p.m. It's best if you ask about the current bus times once you arrive at the bus terminal of Cuenca.

Usually, it rains in Cajas past 1 p.m. (it's a wetland area after all) and therefore better go early.

I took the bus at 10.20 a.m. for $2 (plus a 10 cents terminal fee, which you have to pay at a machine in front of the gate).

The bus ride offers wonderful views and takes about 50 minutes.

Register in the left building (I am not sure why, as I didn't need to sign out when I came back and so they wouldn't have realized if I got lost anyway).
In the right building, you find a restaurant with basic food and toilets.

If you just want an easy hike and see the scenery, first go down to the left and take in the view over the lake from the viewing platform. Then, walk down the path so that you walk around the lake on the right side. Once you arrive on the foot of the mountain, you can choose how far you want to walk around the mountain before turning back.

If you feel adventurous and have good hiking/trekking shoes you can attempt tour number 2 (3 to 4 hours). It will surely give you the most stunning views, but it involves climbing on slippery terrain and should only be done if you can deal with heights.

Tour 2 also starts to the left via the viewing platform. You then continue to the left, climbing across hilly terrain until you reach the main road. Walk along the road for 700 m until you find the starting point of route 2 with green arrows. Now, you are on smoother terrain but watch your step as this is a wetland and you might soak your foot in a swamp.

When you reach the base of the mountain, a 400 m climb lies ahead of you. Take it slowly and try to breathe steadily (it's difficult on 4000 m). The grass was slippery, and I needed my hands to pull myself up further. The area is very exposed and would be dangerous in rain (it rains often here). Therefore, better wear good hiking shoes.

At the top, you are rewarded with spectacular views over black lagoons and green mountains.

You climb down the other side of the mountain which is also slippery and dangerous as there was no clear path and you have to find your own way. Also, I was pressured by the approaching storm in the background.

I made it down just in time before the pouring rain came. The area still was beautiful though and I enjoyed walking across the small bridges.

To get back to Cuenca catch a bus at the bus stop along the road in front of the parking lot which heads in the direction of Cuenca. There is one every hour and it costs $2.

Montañita

This is the most famous backpacker place along the Ecuadorian coast. Apart from a long stretch of beach with great waves for beginner surfers, it offers good ceviche and great party life.

If you are an advanced surfer, you should check out Ayampe or Mompiche. However, they are sleepy small towns and if you are a solo traveler, it might be too quiet for you. Hence, you should give Montañita a try even if you don't want to party all the time. This place can grow on you. It happened to me.

When I first arrived, it was a misty and cold winter day. All I saw were the hundreds of colorful beach chairs and buildings and shops which advertise cheap alcohol. I thought, how could anyone want to stay here, if there are much nicer stretches of sand up and down the coast? However, the next day I got up for surfing and the waves were great. Moreover, the beach is empty until 10 a.m. every morning and if you come before that you can have the whole 3 km to yourself. In the evenings, the atmosphere is very nice as well. You can party if you want to, but you can avoid it if you want a quiet evening.

In town, people greet you and you soon feel like a local. Perhaps, that's why people like to stay for several weeks and grab the chance of taking cheap Spanish classes. Ecuador has a lot of treasures to offer but it was hard to leave Montañita in order to explore more and I think it might enchant you in the same way.

What to do in Montañita

Although it's a small town, this place has a lot of activities to offer.

Learn Spanish in Montañita

Attending a Spanish course in Montañita is a very common thing to do as they probably offer some of the best prices in South America. Since half of the tourists are at the Spanish school you will make friends quickly. You can pre-book classes online (www.montanitaspanishschool.com/) but since packages usually are more expensive you could also ask around once you are there.

Surf in Montañita

For beginners, Montañita is a perfect place to learn how to surf. It's a safe beach break with consistent white water. The green waves are a bit challenging but good for intermediate or advanced surfers. If you get bored, take your board on a bus or in a taxi to head to the neighboring beaches or join a surfari with the surf schools at the beach. Prices for the board and wetsuit are pretty much the same everywhere along the beach: $5/hour, $8/2 hours, $10 per day.

Go whale watching in Puerto Lopez

Puerto Lopez is located 1 hour north of Montañita. Of course, you could also stay there and book a whale watching trip for $25. However, Puerto Lopez is just a harbor with many small fishing boats and therefore not a nice beach to spend time at. Yet, even if you only go on a whale watching tour in Puerto Lopez, be sure to eat a ceviche at the fish market. It was the best ceviche I had in South America and only cost $4.

From Montañita you can book whale watching tours for $30 (for example with *Go Montañita*, June to September). During my tour, we saw a mother and a baby humpback whale. They were very active and jumping several times.

Take a day trip to Isla de la Plata

This is called "Galapagos for the poor" as the island is populated by many animals that also live on the Galapagos.

In case you can't make it to the amazing Galapagos, be sure to do this day trip and at least get a picture of blue-footed boobies. Tours leave from Puerto Lopez but can also be booked from Montañita for $55. If you go during the whale season you might also see jumping humpback whales on the way to and from the island.

Relax in a hammock

Many hostels have a nice outdoor area to relax in hammocks in the evening or during the day when it's too hot (November to February) or rainy. I stayed at **Hidden House** and was very happy there. It was clean and the beds were comfortable. Since my dorm was set close to the street, I didn't hear the music from the bar too much and slept very well.

Walk to the viewpoint

To the side toward Puerto Lopez along the beach of Montañita, there is a viewpoint from which you have a nice view across the ocean and down on the neighboring beach. Sometimes, you can even spot whales in the distance.

Dance until you drop

From Wednesday to Saturday, you can choose between many parties in the clubs and bars of Montañita. It's mostly electro music but also some reggaeton. From Sunday to Tuesday, it's pretty quiet in Montañita though.

Where to eat in Montañita

Montañita has quite a few expensive touristy places, however, you can also eat delicious seafood for really cheap and some other local specialties.

Try encebollado

If you haven't tried this soup with fish, onions, and lime so far, here is the place to do it. You find them in restaurants or at encebollado carts in the center of town (starting at $2.50 including chifle (banana chips). They swear that it's good if you are hungover. However, I also just liked the taste of it.

The best burrito in town

There is a TexMex shack right next to the bridge at the corner of the road that leads to *Hidden House*. At $4 you can have a very delicious burrito with either guacamole or hummus. What's even better is that it comes with French fries that are very crispy (hard to find in South America).

Enjoy a ceviche with sea view

If you walk along the beach between 10 a.m. and 5 p.m. you will spot the yellow ceviche carts (I really liked *Ceviche de Manuel*). Prices start at $6 and include a lot of lime and cilantro and a package of chifle (banana chips). The seafood is fresh and delicious.

Tigrillo for breakfast

Also along the road to *Hidden House* you find a breakfast shack in which I had a dish called Tigrillo. It was cooked and mashed plantains with good feta cheese and an egg with juice for $2.50.

If you crave something sweet

There is a bakery which is marked on maps.me (located opposite of a pizzeria on the first busy street that runs parallel to the ocean) where you can buy the most delicious chocolate croissants for $1. I, unfortunately, can't give you the address because Montañita is so small and exact addresses don't seem to exist on the smaller streets. But it's worth looking for this place as the chocolate inside the croissants is divine and the croissants were always nicely warm. Once I found out about this place, I went back every day.

A trip to the Cuyabeno Rainforest

A trip to the Amazon rainforest is a highlight for many travelers. There are well-known tour options in Colombia, Peru, and of course Brazil. But did you know that Ecuador also has nature reserves where you can observe the pink dolphins, anacondas, monkeys, sloths, and interact with local people? Welcome to Cuyabeno reserve!

I thought about doing a tour to the rainforest for several weeks. I wanted to see the monkeys, colorful frogs, and dolphins; however, I am terribly afraid of spiders. Of which there apparently are many, including tarantulas. In the end, I decided to give it a go because everyone else I talked to had enjoyed their trip to Cuyabeno. I booked a 3n/4d tour at **Cuyabeno Lodge** (https://cuyabenolodge.com.ec/), the first Lodge there used to be in this reserve. Now you can choose between 14.

Best time to visit

Cuyabeno reserve is best to be visited at the end of the rainy season from April to July. During the dry season, once the water is gone, the lodges will close until the lagoons are filled from the rain again. This can be anytime between November and January.

How to get to Lago Agrio

Our meeting point was at 9.30 a.m. at *De Mario Hotel* in Lago Agrio. Since I came the long land route from Colombia, I spent the night before the tour in Lago Agrio. The hotels are basic and cheaper if you search them on Google and book via their website directly or simply walk around town and ask (during daylight) as not many of the accommodations are listed on booking.com.

Lago Agrio isn't a town you want to spend a lot of time in, but I was glad I didn't start the tour after a 5-hour night bus from Quito (leaves at 11 p.m. from Carcelen), as most people in my group did.

The other option is to take a flight with TAME from Quito. However, they often aren't on time, and you might miss part of your first day in the jungle.

My tour at Cuyabeno Lodge

Following I recount my tour in detail, so that you can decide for yourself, whether this would be an adventure you would enjoy.

The driver showed up shortly before 9.30 a.m. and we boarded a bus which would bring us to Cuyabeno Lodge. First, however, we drove to the airport to pick up the rest of the group. After waiting for an hour, the driver informed us that the plane wouldn't arrive until after lunchtime. Hence, he would wait for them and the 5 of us would be brought to Cuyabeno in a different car. We switched the luggage onto the new vehicle and 2.5 hours later arrived at the river.

We had a basic lunch of rice and chicken with a slice of watermelon before boarding the motorized canoe. They made sure that our backpacks were well covered with a plastic wrap, and we all received a rain poncho that we could keep until the end of our stay. Luckily, we didn't need the ponchos but apparently, it had rained the previous 3 days.

The ride in the canoe was great because you are surrounded by so much green and navigate from a broad, milky brown river to small, black channels.

Excitement rose when we spotted monkeys (3 kinds), two sloths, two toucans flying high above us across the jungle, and a small anaconda!

We reached the Cuyabeno Lodge at about 4.30 p.m. and were welcomed with a freshly made lemonade (some ants in the glass, but you better quickly get used to that as ants, spiders, and frogs will be your constant companions).

We were shown to our rooms and could settle in. At 5.30 p.m. was our next meeting point. We all were handed a paddle and this time boarded a canoe without a motor.
It was beautiful to paddle out onto Laguna Grande in the purple hue of the setting sun.
In the middle of the lagoon, it's safe to swim, and the ones who felt up for it could take a refreshing dip.

After returning, we had some time to relax in the hammock area or could get a coffee, tea or fruit from the free food station that's set up all day.
Plus, it was a good time to plug in the cameras or phones in the plugs in the hammock area, since there were no sockets in the room.

It was nice to hang out with my group as we got along well and had many entertaining conversations.

Dinner was pork meat in a sauce with salad and yuca. For dessert we had a pineapple tart. Food generally was "muy rico" (very good).

The night

Well, there are mosquito nets, but still, I was afraid that the spider I saw on the wall of my bathroom would crawl across my face during the night. So, I woke up a few times but probably, it was more because of my paranoia, and nothing would actually have come through the net.

At least, I didn't have three huge frogs in my room (or toilet) as all my other group members did. If you can't deal with frogs or spiders, you probably won't enjoy your stay in the rainforest. You just have to believe the locals who say that they are harmless and hope that they will stay away from you in the shower or the bed.

Day 2

I woke up early to the many sounds of the jungle. That's one of the highlights around here as some bird calls are simply strange. It's very enjoyable to just listen to nature.

So, soon, I couldn't stay in bed anymore because I wanted to see who these sounds belonged to.

I climbed the lookout tower of Cuyabeno Lodge (after getting a tea and a banana) and found 4 monkeys in the tree right next to the tower. A hummingbird paid a visit as well. Plus, I saw some other bright, yellow birds fly by.

After breakfast, we received rubber boots and set out for a walk in the forest. My feelings switched from disgust because we had to climb around spider webs to excitement because we learned about different trees and spotted frogs from tiny to big (that looked like leaves), and a praying mantis.

Lunch was at 1.30 p.m. and consisted of corn with cheese, fried plantain with beef stew (delicious), salad, and rice. Dessert was a bowl of strawberries.

Then, it was nap time until 4.30 p.m. while listening to the jungle. When the sun is out, it gets stifling hot here.

So, in the early evening, we set out for a boat ride. We found the river dolphins and watched them appearing and disappearing for a while, plus saw some more birds. During sunset, we again had the option to swim in the lagoon.

Dinner was vegetable soup, a delicious fish with yuca fries and vegetables.

Later, we met at the dock again to set out for a night boat ride in search of Caymans. Twice, we saw the reflection of their eyes in our lamps, but they always dove away. However, we found two small snakes. Yet, the best thing about the night boat ride was looking at the sky full of stars. Since there is hardly any light pollution out here, you can spot the milky way very clearly. So, it's a good idea to go up on the lookout tower during nighttime and watch the stars.

Day 3

After breakfast (consisting of granola, yogurt, fresh bread, butter, and jam), we boarded a two-hour boat ride to spot more monkeys and to visit one of the four communities living in the Cuyabeno Reserve. We visited the family of our guide, and it was nice to have this personal touch to it.

We didn't see much of the village though as we only came for a cooking class. This activity was one of my highlights of

this tour. We got to try fresh sugar cane and prepared a casabe, which is a dough made of yuca (like the Brazilian Tapioca).

We cut the yuca branches in the garden to pull out the yuca roots.
We pealed and washed them. Afterward, we grated them until it looked like grated cheese.

The wife of our guide then squeezed out all the water with a "towel" woven of plants and a wooden stick.

Afterward, we sieved the now dry yuca flour and used the yuca milk as a hand cream. My hands had never been so smooth!

It was time to fry the flour. We simply put it on a big, hot, pizza shaped pan and after a while, the flour stuck together on its own.

Right away, we could enjoy it with tuna or jam. Delicious!

The way back took some time and once we arrived at Cuyabeno Lodge we were all hungry for lunch again, which was a well-marinated beef steak with beans, rice, and vegetables. Dessert was a peach in cream.

It was another hot afternoon and hammock time until 4.30 p.m. when we set out in a paddle canoe. It was nice to enjoy the tranquility while watching some birds. For sunset, we paddled to Laguna Grande to take a swim and observe a beautiful sunset.

Back at shore, we put our jungle boots on, brought our lamps or phones and set out on a night walk. That was not pleasant for me, but it sure was thrilling. We saw huge spiders, one of them poisonous. Two tarantulas, two scorpions, and a snake. Unfortunately, we didn't see any colorful, poisonous frogs, which I would have liked to see, but so, I was glad when we reached the boat and weren't on the spider filled forest path anymore.

Dinner was chicken in a sauce with rice and vegetables, plus a pumpkin soup.

After dinner, we wanted to go watch the stars on the lookout tower, however, our climb to the top was stopped by a small boa who also used the railing of the stairs as her path. Oh well, better to go to bed anyway, since we'd have an early bird-watching boat ride the next morning.

Day 4

We met at the dock at 6 a.m. and were blessed with a boat ride full of toucans and parrots, while the sun was hiding behind clouds.

We returned to the lodge for the last breakfast and after packing our bags had another hour until the boat would bring us back to civilization.

I made use of the time to go up to the lookout tower and got to see two kinds of toucans from up close, while they were eating and a green parrot. That's why I came to the rainforest. To see animals, that I wouldn't see anywhere else in their natural habitat.

Conclusion

Except for the colorful frogs, we saw all the animals I wanted to see and had a great time preparing the casabe bread. The trip was a success and definitely an adventurous experience.

Yet, if like me, you don't like spiders, you have to know that this is the animal you will see most and come closest with. Right after that follow the frogs in the bathroom... So, mentally prepare yourself for that and you can enjoy the views of the landscape that is flooded by water, the bright night sky, the monkeys, and the many colorful, and loud birds.

Where to book a trip to Cuyabeno Lodge

You best book it right through their website: http://cuyabenolodge.com.ec/. Three nights/four days in a dorm cost $310. This is the best price I found from the lodges. The programs of all the lodges are very similar.

Border crossing: From Ecuador to Peru

I traveled from Cuenca to Mancora. Unfortunately, there was no day bus available but getting to Peru was an easy night bus ride away. You can travel with *Azuray* or *Super Semeria* and it makes sense to get to a city that is 7 to 10 hours away, like Mancora or Piura.

I took the Super Semeria for $18 at 10.30 p.m.
Before the border, they checked our luggage and I had to open my backpack.
Then, they stored the bags in the trunk again and we later got off at the immigration building with just our hand luggage. First, we got the exit stamp of Ecuador and then the entry stamp to Peru. The process was quick and easy.
A 5 minutes' drive down the road, the police came on the bus again and we had to show our passports and luggage once more, but after that, we were driving on Peruvian roads for good.

We arrived in the calm beach town of Mancora at 5 a.m. where we took a tuk-tuk to the hostel for $1. I was lucky that I could check in and already use my bed.

It's also easy to catch a day or night bus from **Guayaquil** to Mancora or Piura.

Well, normally it's easy. However, on the day I arrived in Mancora (lucky me), the gasoline strike started in Ecuador and the borders remained closed for two weeks. Chaos broke out in the cities of Ecuador and tourists were stuck wherever they were. I never expected anything like that to happen as I had had such a wonderful time in Ecuador and didn't have any reason to feel unsafe. It seemed like a stable country, and it made me sad that things can go downhill so fast. Of course, with covid we sadly are used to border closures even more now. I hope that countries can solve future issues in a better way and that tourism can resume just as I experienced it. Ecuador is an amazing, diverse country that should be put on your travel list.

Border Crossing: Ecuador to Colombia at Ipiales

If you want to take the scenic land route from Quito or Otavalo to Colombia, you have to prepare yourselves for about 16 hours of bus rides until you reach bigger cities. If you want to travel from Colombia to Ecuador (Cali to Quito), you do everything in reverse.

1. Step: Quito to Tulcan

Board a bus at Carcelen bus station in Quito toward Tulcan. The same bus will also leave Quitumbe station one hour earlier, but you will just spend the first hour driving around in the city of Quito. The journey to Tulcan costs $7.25-$10.25 and takes 5-7 hours. Buses leave hourly or sometimes even more often.

It is also possible to board the bus to Tulcan in Otavalo, from where it takes 3 - 4 hours.

2. Step: Ecuadorian exit stamp

From the bus station in Tulcan, you have no other option but taking a taxi to the border for $3.50. If there are other people, you can share it with them. Tell the driver that you need to get off at the Ecuadorian immigration in order to get your exit stamp. Since there were hardly any other people (at about 2 p.m.), I had my stamp in two minutes.

3. Step: Colombian entry stamp

Then, I walked the 200 m to the Colombian border office. Many people were lurking around in front of the building which felt a bit sketchy, but I could walk straight to the entrance and had my entry stamp 3 minutes later. So, no difficulties at all at this border crossing (no questions asked about return flight tickets, which I didn't have).

4. Step: Colectivo into Ipiales

Walk back to the parking lot in front of the Colombian border building. There, you can take a colectivo to the bus station of Ipiales for $1 or 3900 COP.
The main reason why it's worth to do this border crossing comes now: visit the beautiful monastery of Las Lajas. It looks like an enchanted castle, set in a green valley with waterfalls.

Visit Las Lajas monastery

The colectivos which go to Las Lajas are waiting on the parking lot above the bus station in Ipiales. They leave when they are full, take 20 minutes and cost 2500 COP.

Leave your luggage in your hotel or at the luggage storage at the bus station as you have to walk quite a number of stairs to get to the monastery from the parking lot. The walk takes about 15 minutes and leads past hundreds of souvenir shops.

The visit of the monastery grounds or entering the church is free. At about 6.30 p.m. they turn on the lights which let the monastery shimmer in blue or purple. Hence, I recommend spending a night in Ipiales.

Journey from Ipiales to Pasto, Popayan, or Cali

The next three cities north of the border where it might be worth to spend a night or even a few days are Pasto, Popayan, and Cali. However, it's not recommended to travel on any of these roads after dark. Between Ipiales and Popayan you curve along mountain passes and accidents can be deadly pretty quickly. I traveled with *Transpiales* during the day. We didn't have any problems and the movies on the bus were alright, too. We only had one restaurant stop at 2 p.m., so bring snacks.

My bus from Ipiales to Cali cost 40k COP and took 12 hours. It takes 2 hours to get to Pasto and 8 hours to Popayan.

Be careful with the food or fruit juice from the bus station. I was sick for my first three days in Colombia, and I think it was from the juice we received with the almuerzo at the bus station somewhere along the road.

Border Crossing: Colombia to Ecuador at Mocoa (La Hormiga/Lago Agrio)

If you want to cross from Colombia to Ecuador by land, whichever border you choose it means many hours spent on the bus. In case you are visiting the Cuyabeno rainforest in Ecuador and you like watching the landscape through a bus window, it might make sense that you travel via this border. Popayan is the last big city along this route.

First step: Popayan – Pitalito - Mocoa

Since there were no clear indications when buses to Pitalito were leaving, I simply arrived at the bus station at about 8a.m. *Cootrans Laboyana* talked me into buying a ticket with them but in hindsight, I wished I had talked to some more agencies before buying the ticket and that I had chosen another one. I bought a ticket directly to Mocoa at 9.15 a.m. for 55k as they said that would be the soonest bus. We were supposed to arrive at 6 p.m. However, their van vas very late and several buses from *Cootranshuila* had left to Pitalito meanwhile. We finally took off at 10.50 a.m.

The view of green hills during the drive was beautiful and probably not as dangerous as the road from Ipiales to Popayan because the cliffs weren't very high. However, for the most part, it was a bumpy gravel road, and you could only drive stop and go at 20 km/h. Still, we crossed a tipped over bus from our bus company. Luckily, the people weren't hurt but had to wait on the side of the road.

As soon as the good road started again, we stopped at a restaurant for 20 minutes.

We finally reached Pitalito at 5 p.m. The last minivan of the day from the same company going to Mocoa had already left, so I got moved to a different van. That wouldn't have been a problem but of course, there were no more good seats and only one in the back squeezed in between smelly, big men.

So, best book your trip to Mocoa in two legs and only buy your ticket to Pitalito first (with the next reliable bus that leaves). Then, you can choose your seats on the next bus or minivan from Pitalito to Mocoa.

Instead of driving the remaining 3 hours straight to Mocoa we stopped for 30 minutes at a restaurant at 7 p.m. We also were stopped twice by police or the army and had to leave the car so that they could search it. At least that only took 5 to 10 minutes each time.

By now it was dark. Exactly what I wanted to avoid on those curvy, bad roads and I strongly recommend that you cover any distance South of Popayan during daylight.

After dinner, we had to stop for another 30 minutes in the middle of nowhere because two trucks got stuck next to each other. At least many other cars were forced to wait as well and so we weren't alone.

We finally arrived in Mocoa at 9.15 p.m., and they were already shouting that the next van to La Hormiga was about to leave. So, you could travel even closer to the border until quite late (the first buses start at 4 a.m.).

I was glad to finally be at my destination for the night though. I took a taxi to my hotel although it was only 600 m to walk. I wasn't sure how safe this place was at night. Luckily, some restaurants were still open.

Second Step: Mocoa – La Hormiga – Puente Internacional

The next morning, I went back to the bus station at 10.20 a.m. and was lucky that the next van to the border was leaving in 10 minutes. We even left on time and were traveling quite quickly (no seatbelts, of course).

We reached La Hormiga at 1.45 p.m. where I had to change onto a jeep that would bring us to the border (puente internacional). We waited until it was filled up and then drove to the border while picking up and dropping off some people along the way.

We finally reached the border at 3.15 p.m. The trip from Mocoa until here cost 37k COP.

When I climbed out of the jeep there was a local who offered to exchange pesos to dollars, and I was happy to hear that he had the same exchange rate as the good ATMs.

Third step: Bus to immigration - Pass immigration and taxi or bus into Lago Agrio

Then, I had to walk 200 m to cross the river. I now had entered Ecuador, but I hadn't yet passed an immigration building. To get there, I boarded a bus for 50 cents which drove us the 2 kilometers to the immigration offices.

The counters of Colombia and Ecuador are located next to each other. First, get your exit stamp and after that, your entry stamp into the new country.

It took less than 10 minutes as there only were three other people in the building.

Then, you have to go back to where the bus from the border dropped you off, to catch the next one into Lago Agrio. I made the mistake to wait at the exit of the Ecuadorian side and the following bus just drove by without stopping. Since it was quite hot, I then opted for a green-white taxi which drove me directly to my hotel in 20 minutes for 2 USD.

So, like my experience from Ipiales to Cali, getting to the border of San Miguel/Lago Agrio hadn't been any easier. I thought it would be a good option for me because I was starting a rainforest tour in Cuyabeno, and this way wouldn't have to fly to Quito and then take the night bus from Quito to get here. However, it's safer to fly and would be quicker and more agreeable.

Bonus Chapter: The Galapagos Islands

The islands which are famous for their abundant wild-life can be reached in a 1.5 to 2 hours flight from mainland Ecuador. The special thing about the Galapagos is that all the islands are within the environmentally protected national park. It's forbidden to touch, feed, hunt or interact with the animals closer than two meters. This resulted in the animals not paying any attention to the visitors and simply going about their business. You can walk in the middle of a colony of sea lions and see their natural behavior. The same goes for many kinds of iguanas, colorful birds like the blue-footed boobie, and much more. Underwater you can see sea horses, sharks (e.g. hammerhead), whales, etc. It's a paradise for divers and best to be explored on a liveaboard trip. To be honest, they are very expensive but since it's probably a once in a lifetime experience you should seriously consider it if you come to this part of the world.

Apart from that, you can also visit the main animal spots on day trips (without an expensive cruise), and with everything included, your trip will come to about $100 - $150 per day. Following you can read about the different options.

How to get to the Galapagos

You can fly to **Baltera** airport on Santa Cruz (the main city is Puerto Ayora) or to **San Cristobal** from Guayaquil. Before you even check in your bags you have to buy a tourist pass for $20. Then, they will check your bags thoroughly for whether you bring any food or animal products. They will do the same again once you land on the Galapagos Islands. They let me keep my dry snacks like cookies and chocolate though.

When you go through customs, along with receiving your Galapagos stamp you have to pay $100 for the national park.

How to get from the airports into the city center

I think the best option is to fly into San Cristobal and out of Baltera.

San Cristobal is pretty small, and you can walk from the airport into town (or take a taxi for $1.50). There is a huge sea lion colony living there as well. Therefore, you can check off shooting selfies with them from your bucket list right on your first day.

104

If you arrive or leave from Baltera

From Baltera airport you have to take a bus to a small ocean channel (20 minutes). Tickets cost $5. Then, you take a 5min ferry ride for $1 to cross the channel. On the other side, you either take a taxi for $25 for up to four people or a bus for $5 for 30-40 minutes. The bus will drop you off at the bus station outside of Puerto Ayora and you need another taxi for $1.50 to get to the city center.

To reach the airport from the city center (Puerto Ayora) the cheapest option to get to the channel is a shared taxi for $7 per person. From the other side of the channel, you then again take the bus for $5.

What to see on Santa Cruz

Puerto Ayora is a very touristy town with many ocean-themed restaurants. You can find a seafood walking street from 6 p.m. to 10 p.m. where the top thing to try is fresh lobster.

Fish market

If you want to see sea lions or pelicans, go to the small seafood market where they sell the catch of the day. Lobster season is from mid-August to mid-January.

Seafood street

This is the busiest place in the evening, and you can find all kinds of seafood and some other dishes. Lobster starts at $20.

Charles Darwin Research Center

This center is located a straightforward 20 mins walk from town. You can read about their projects to save the tortoises and other animals on Galapagos and can have a look at the baby tortoises and some older ones. They are all in safe cages and if you travel around the Galapagos Islands you will see the giant tortoises in the wild. However, you can't find any baby tortoises in the wild and hence this center is worth a visit. On top of that, the displays are made quite well. The entry fee used to be free but since 2022 they charge $10 to see the turtles.

Tortuga Bay Beach

This beach is a paradise if the weather is good! 1.5 km of white sand and light blue waves with clear water. It's possible to surf there but you have to bring your board from town. Renting a board is about $30 per day. The walk to Tortuga Bay is a well-kept boardwalk past cactuses and takes about 40 minutes. It's 2.5 km from the entrance hut to the surf beach and then another kilometer along the beach to get to a safe swimming bay. That small bay is also very picturesque with blue water lined by mangroves.

If you don't want to walk you can take a 20-minutes water taxi for $10 one way.

Salt flat and Las Grietas

This place is an 80-cent water taxi from the port and then a 15-minutes' walk past a small beach and the salt flats. Las Grietas is a gorge with clear water (not much to see though). If you have time, it's a nice walk and swim but it could be skipped without having missed too much.

Lava tunnel in the highlands

This visit was part of our tour and included a visit to the highland tortoise breeding center. That center was nice because the giant tortoises were roaming around the property freely and you could take pictures with empty tortoises' shells. This place you could easily visit with a taxi. I am not sure if you want to visit the lava tunnel without a guide as it's mostly a big, dark tunnel with two parts where you have to crawl or rob on your stomach. It was, however, a cool experience to be below the hardened lava instead of walking on top of the tunnel-like at all the other places we visited.

Take the ferry to another island

From Puerto Ayora you can take a speed boat to Isabela for $25 to $30 each way (at 7 a.m. or 2 p.m. and it takes about 2.5 hours). To San Cristobal for $30 (also at 7 a.m. and 2 p.m. / 2 hours) or book organized day trips to Española or Floreana.

If you travel on the speed ferry beware that it's a very bumpy ride. It's very loud from the motor and you might get wet or sit in the sun. Therefore, bring:
- a rain jacket,
- sunscreen,
- something to cover your head that doesn't fly off,
- something to drink,
- a snack, and
- earplugs or headphones (to listen to music and pass the time. You can't do much more than that because everything will fly out of your hands during the bumps).

What to see on San Cristobal

This was our favorite island to stay on as it offered a good infrastructure without seeming too touristy. Just by walking around you will see many sea lions, blue-footed boobies, and marine iguanas.

Snorkel at Muelle Tijeretas

It's a nice 40-minutes' walk from town to get to this rocky bay. Along the path, you will pass the small-town beaches with the sea lions going about their business and the interpretation center, which wasn't very good but there were toilets.

Tijeretas is perfect for snorkeling. In the clear water, I saw several turtles, many different fish, and marine iguanas.

It's also nice to enjoy the view from the viewpoint.

On the way back you could walk to Punta Carola, which is a pretty beach with more sea lions and many turtles. If you snorkel there you will surely encounter a playful sea lion in the water.

Snorkel at Playa Loberia

This beach is located past the airport. Either it takes 50 minutes to walk there or a quick $3 taxi ride. It's nice to visit if you haven't yet snorkeled a lot on Galapagos or haven't seen many beaches. However, if you are short on time, you can skip this.

Dive at Kicker Rock

A two-tank dive trip costs $150. From December to March, you have a big chance to see many hammerhead sharks. Whitetip and blacktip reef sharks, you can see all the time (also at many other spots on the Galapagos and while snorkeling).

Isabela Island

This island is shaped like a sea horse and a big variety of animals live on and around it. If you stay on Isabela, you can spend some time at the 3 km long, white beach, and watch blue-footed boobies fishing at *El Estero*. Another nice lookout point along the way is *Playa del Amor*.

On Isabela, there is another **tortoise sanctuary** from which you can walk across a boardwalk to spot **flamingos** in the wetlands.

All those places are best reached by bicycle.

A popular tour is to **hike to the rim of the volcano** on Isabela, however, it's hard to get clear views and if you have more time in South America, there are better volcanoes to be explored.

The highlights on Isabela are the tours to *Tintoreras* and Los *Tuneles*.

Los Tuneles

Los Tuneles lies a 1.5-hour speedboat ride from Isabela. On the way, you have the chance to spot whales and dolphins. At Tuneles, which are rock arches close above the seawater, you can see sea horses. Don't look for tiny creatures, though... They are more than 10 centimeters tall and pretty thick!
There are only two boats that visit Tuneles every day and spots are sold out quickly, even though this half-day snorkel tour costs $120-$140. It's expensive, yes, but it was one of my favorite spots on the Galapagos.

Tintoreras

This snorkeling spot is located right in front of Isabela (10-minute boat ride). The cool thing about it is that there is a channel to which whitetip sharks come to rest. We saw 25 when we were there and apparently, that is rather a low number.
During the snorkel activity, we saw several eagle rays, a marble ray, penguins, turtles, and sea lions.

DIY trip on the Galapagos Islands

Now, you know about all the places you can and should visit on a DIY trip to the Galapagos. I suggest 2-3 nights on Isabela, Santa Cruz, and San Cristobal. After 10 days on the Galapagos, you will surely be satisfied because you feel like you have seen everything. At about $1300 for 10 days, it's doable to explore this amazing place.

Last-minute cruises vs. pre-booked cruises

A cruise around the Galapagos is the perfect way to see the islands and many different snorkel spots. First of all, you don't have to deal with the bumpy, uncomfortable speed boat rides between the islands, and secondly, it's just nice to live on a boat for a few days, call it your home, always have the ocean around you (chance to spot whales and dolphins), and see the milky way and thousands of stars at night. Thirdly, you can only visit some parts of the Galapagos on a cruise (backside of Isabela and the famous dive spots Darwin and Wolf).

The good thing about pre-booking a cruise is that you can choose the ship and route you will be on for sure. The bad thing is that you won't find anything below $2200.

Last minute cruise on the Galapagos

I did an 8-day last-minute cruise for $1500. I had an amazing time; however, I would do a few things differently now about the last-minute booking process. I think the perfect balance of seeing the Galapagos is a 5-day cruise to the backside of Isabela or a cruise to Darwin and Wolf and then visit the rest of the islands with DIY island hopping.

What you have to know about booking a last-minute cruise is that most boats depart from Baltera Airport (not the harbor in the city), therefore, you might have to do the annoying trip to Baltera Airport to get to your cruise, after booking it in the center of town. Make sure that they include the taxi transport to the channel or walk to a different booking office. It's worth it to compare prices but *Agencia GalapSurfIslands* at the bend in the road near the fish market seemed to have the best prices (as well as *Bridmartours S.A.* near the fish food street).

If you have a certain route in mind, check online when the boats depart for those routes and get to Santa Cruz a day or two before. It seemed like many boats departed on Friday and Saturday.

The cheapest boat (Golondrina) with tiny two bunk bed cabins will cost around $1350 for **8 days**. If you share the cabin with someone you know, it's okay, otherwise, it's a very small cabin and you only want to be in there to sleep. The *Golondrina* usually travels together with the *Fragata* and sometimes, people are lucky to get bumped up onto Fragata, which is a bit more spacious.

A medium-class boat will cost you $1150 to $1500 for a **five-day** trip and one with a jacuzzi about $1800.

My favorite places on my cruise

I really liked **Fernandina Island** on the backside of Isabela because it was nice to snorkel, and we saw an orca for about 2 seconds. They are not there a lot, but you might get lucky and sit on a dinghy boat 3 m from an orca hunting a turtle.

The prettiest island was **Chinese Hat** with white beaches, blue water, red soil, and green plants. What an amazing color mix.

The best snorkeling activity we had on **Rabida Island**, where we saw many fish, sea lions, sharks, turtles, and rays.

Things to know before coming to the Galapagos

It's a remote place but if you know about the following things before coming here, you will have a truly wonderful time.

Cash is king

You can't pay with credit cards anywhere on the Galapagos or if you can, there will be a high additional fee. So, if you buy a cruise for several thousand dollars, that means several trips to the ATM. There are ATMs on the three bigger islands, and they have different withdrawal limits and costs. The best ATM I found had a limit of $600 and a cost of $4.50.

The Wi-Fi sucks

Research and download everything you need before you come to the Galapagos. I somehow forgot to download maps.me for the Galapagos and couldn't download the 30mb during the 10 days even if I turned on mobile data. Hence, prepare for a holiday without internet except for a few WhatsApp messages.

Rent a wet suit

Unfortunately, the water here goes from cold to freezing. I felt like my brain froze several times during snorkeling. Even with the long wet suits we only managed to stay in the water for 30-40 minutes, although there always was so much to see. Snorkeling right off the beaches of Santa Cruz and San Cristobal was doable without a wet suit though.

Pack for windy, rainy, hot, and cold weather

Especially if you do a cruise, you will encounter windy weather but, on the islands, it also quickly changes between the blazing sun and a wet drizzle. Therefore, pack the following things apart from the usual traveling gear:

- rain jacket (also good against the wind)
- warm sweater or down jacket
- long pants
- socks
- beanie (for the nights in the boat cabin with too much a/c)
- sunscreen

Whether you choose an organized cruise or a DIY trip on the Galapagos, you will have an amazing time. The same goes for Ecuador in general. Somehow, the country is very underrated and merits more tourists who discover the huge variety of things to see and do.

Some useful words in Spanish

English	Spanish
Hello	Hola
How are you?	¿Cómo estás?
I'm well and you?	Bien, gracias y tú?
Where are you from?	¿De donde eres?
I'm from...	Soy de..(los Estados Unidos, Inglaterra)
Yes	Si
No	No
Where is the toilet/ATM?	¿Dónde está el baño/cajero?
Thank you.	Gracias
How much is...?	¿Cuánto cuesta...?
Sorry	Lo siento
Please	Por favor
I need to change money.	Necesito cambiar dinero.
I would like...	Me gustaría... / Quiero...
The bill please.	La cuenta, por favor.
Water	Agua
Chicken	Pollo
Without meat	Sin carne
Enjoy your meal.	Buen provecho.
What time does... arrive?	¿Cuándo llegará...?
Bus	El autobús
Plane	El avión
Boat	El barco
Waterfall	La cascada
Right	Derecha
Left	Izquierda

Do you need more info?

In case you need more info, I am happy to help. Contact or follow me through these channels. Especially on Instagram, you can enjoy daily travel tips, inspiration, and travel quotes.

(b) www.swissmissontour.com

(i) @swissmissontour

(f) SwissMissOnTour

(w) www.slgigerbooks.wordpress.com

By the way, since the photos in this travel guide are black and white, you can send me an e-mail with a picture of the book, and I will send you the e-book version of I love Ecuador for free. In the e-book, the pictures are in color.

Did you like this travel guide?

In case you liked this travel guide, I'd greatly appreciate a positive review on Amazon, and it would be a good support if you told your friends about it 😊

More books by S. L. Giger / SwissMiss onTour

Printed in Great Britain
by Amazon

27439126R00069